TAO WISDOM

道德經

TAO WISDOM

Great Quotes from the Ancient Chinese Way of Virtue

LAO TZU

Amber Books Ltd
United House
North Road
London N7 9DP
United Kingdom
www.amberbooks.co.uk
Facebook: amberbooks
YouTube: amberbooksltd
Instagram: amberbooksltd
X(Twitter): @amberbooks

ISBN: 978-1-83886-642-6

Design & Editorial: Amber Books Ltd
Compiled by Abbie Headon

Printed and bound in China

TRADITIONAL CHINESE BOOKBINDING
This book has been produced using traditional Chinese bookbinding techniques, using a method that was developed during the Ming Dynasty (1368–1644) and remained in use until the adoption of Western binding techniques in the early 1900s. In traditional Chinese binding, single sheets of paper are printed on one side only, and each sheet is folded in half, with the printed pages on the outside. The book block is then sandwiched between two boards and sewn together through punched holes close to the cut edges of the folded sheets.

Editor: Abbie Headon is a writer and editor who has worked across a wide range of publishing roles and genres, including self-help, popular science, memoir, fiction, and humour. Her books include *Poetry First Aid Kit*, *The Power of Yes*, *LEGO Build Yourself Happy* and *The Periodic Table Illustrated.* She is a Bookseller Rising Star and a Fellow of the Royal Society of Arts, and you can find her online at @abbieheadon.

Contents

Introduction

THE ORIGINS OF TAOISM, also known as Daoism, are shrouded in mystery, which is perhaps appropriate for a philosophical and religious tradition that itself resists firm definitions. Its key text, the *Tao Te Ching*, dates from approximately the fourth century BCE, written by a philosopher called Laozi – a name meaning 'Old Master' – about whom not much is known, although several competing accounts of his life place him in different times and locations in ancient China. From its beginnings in China, Taoism has spread around the world, particularly since the late twentieth century. Its teachings can be found in temples, as a religious practice, and also in a wider set of cultural activities including tai chi and meditation.

The word 'Tao' itself can be translated as 'way', 'path', 'road' or 'technique', and describes the flow of nature and the universe. It is hard to define, as the opening verse of the *Tao Te Ching* states: 'The Tao that can be trodden is not the enduring and unchanging Tao. The name that can be named is not the enduring and unchanging name.'

Taoist writings explore how the underlying order of the universe can be a guide for us, and how we might learn to live in harmony with ourselves and the world around us by being more open to it. One key concept in Taoism is *wu wei*, which has various translations including 'non-action' or 'effortless action'. In the natural world, a seed grows into a plant, the plant grows to maturity and then decays back into the earth it came from, all without conscious effort.

In a similar way, we usually perform activities such as breathing, walking or brushing our teeth, all without over-thinking the individual steps required to achieve our goals. And yet in other parts of our lives, obstacles such as stress, fear or anger can take us out of our natural flow, making life harder for us and those around us. To live according to the principle of *wu wei* does not mean to become lazy and inactive; it is more about removing our ego from our decisions and finding a way to flow through life with gentleness.

Another Taoist concept is the balanced pair of forces known as *yin* and *yang*, opposing elements that are permanently connected and related to each other. Taoism teaches us to live in the knowledge that light and dark exist side by side, and within each other. In the words of the *Tao Te Ching*: 'Misery! – happiness is to be found by its side! Happiness! – misery lurks beneath it!'

By accepting a balance of joy and sadness, and approaching life with a natural flow instead of a harsh rigidity, we can live with a more childlike openness and become both wiser and simpler, however paradoxical that might sound. Laozi teaches that 'To know and yet think we do not know is the highest attainment' – and so we can allow ourselves to stay open to the *Tao Te Ching*'s teachings, without demanding full understanding. Just as a wave rolls across the ocean or a stream cascades over its rocky bed without ceasing, the meaning of the Tao is both constant and ever-changing, and cannot be pinned down to a single definition.

精

The Tao that can be trodden is not the enduring and unchanging Tao. The name that can be named is not the enduring and unchanging name.

(Chapter 1:1)

精

A violent wind does not last for a whole morning; a sudden rain does not last for the whole day. To whom is it that these two things are owing? To Heaven and Earth.

(Chapter 23:1)

There was something undefined and complete, coming into existence before Heaven and Earth. How still it was and formless, standing alone, and undergoing no change, reaching everywhere and in no danger of being exhausted! It may be regarded as the Mother of all things.

(Chapter 25:1)

精

All-pervading is the Great Tao!
It may be found on the left hand and on the right.

(Chapter 34:1)

All things under heaven sprang from It as existing and named; that existence sprang from It as non-existent and not named.

(Chapter 40:2)

精

The Tao produced One; One produced Two;
Two produced Three; Three produced All things.

(Chapter 42:1)

精

All things are produced by the Tao, and nourished by its outflowing operation. They receive their forms according to the nature of each, and are completed according to the circumstances of their condition.

(Chapter 51:1)

The Tao which originated all under the sky is to be considered as the mother of them all.

(Chapter 52:1)

無為

The highest excellence is like that of water.
The excellence of water appears in its benefiting all things,
and in its occupying, without striving to the contrary,
the low place which all men dislike.
Hence its way is near to that of the Tao.

(Chapter 8:1)

無為

Who can make the muddy water clear? Let it be still, and it will gradually become clear. Who can secure the condition of rest? Let movement go on, and the condition of rest will gradually arise.

(Chapter 15:3)

When things in the vegetable world have displayed their luxuriant growth, we see each of them return to its root. This returning to their root is what we call the state of stillness; and that stillness may be called a reporting that they have fulfilled their appointed end.

(Chapter 16:1)

無為

Gravity is the root of lightness;
stillness, the ruler of movement.

(Chapter 26:1)

If anyone should wish to get the kingdom for himself, and to effect this by what he does, I see that he will not succeed. The kingdom is a spirit-like thing, and cannot be got by active doing. He who would so win it destroys it; he who would hold it in his grasp loses it.

(Chapter 29:1)

無為

The Tao in its regular course does nothing for the sake of doing it, and so there is nothing which it does not do.

(Chapter 37:1)

無為

The softest thing in the world dashes against and overcomes the hardest; that which has no substantial existence enters where there is no crevice. I know hereby what advantage belongs to doing nothing with a purpose.

(Chapter 43:1)

It is the way of Heaven not to strive, and yet it skilfully overcomes; not to speak, and yet it is skilful in obtaining a reply; does not call, and yet men come to it of themselves.

(Chapter 73:2)

With all the sharpness of the Way of Heaven, it injures not; with all the doing in the way of the sage he does not strive.

(Chapter 81:3)

智慧

It is better to leave a vessel unfilled, than to attempt to carry it when it is full. If you keep feeling a point that has been sharpened, the point cannot long preserve its sharpness.

(Chapter 9:1)

智慧

If we could renounce our sageness and discard our wisdom, it would be better for the people a hundredfold. If we could renounce our benevolence and discard our righteousness, the people would again become filial and kindly.

(Chapter 19:1)

智慧

The sage is always skilful at saving men, and so he does not cast away any man; he is always skilful at saving things, and so he does not cast away anything.

(Chapter 27:1)

智慧

Scholars of the highest class, when they hear about the Tao, earnestly carry it into practice. Scholars of the middle class, when they have heard about it, seem now to keep it and now to lose it. Scholars of the lowest class, when they have heard about it, laugh greatly at it.

(Chapter 41:1)

智慧

For regulating the human in our constitution and rendering the proper service to the heavenly, there is nothing like moderation.

(Chapter 59:1)

智慧

I have three precious things which I prize and hold fast. The first is gentleness; the second is economy; and the third is shrinking from taking precedence of others.

(Chapter 67:2)

智慧

To know and yet think we do not know
is the highest attainment;
not to know and yet think we do know is a disease.

(Chapter 71:1)

智慧

When the people do not fear what they ought to fear,
that which is their great dread will come on them.
Let them not thoughtlessly indulge themselves
in their ordinary life; let them not act as if weary
of what that life depends on.

(Chapter 72:1–2)

智慧

The sage does not accumulate for himself. The more that he expends for others, the more does he possess of his own; the more that he gives to others, the more does he have himself.

(Chapter 81:2)

交流

What all men fear is indeed to be feared;
but how wide and without end is the range of questions
asking to be discussed!

(Chapter 20:1)

交流

Music and dainties will make the passing guest stop for a time. But though the Tao as it comes from the mouth seems insipid and has no flavour, though it seems not worth being looked at or listened to, the use of it is inexhaustible.

(Chapter 35:2)

交流

The Tao is hidden, and has no name; but it is the Tao which is skilful at imparting to all things what they need and making them complete.

(Chapter 41:3)

交流

There are few in the world who attain to the teaching without words, and the advantage arising from non-action.

(Chapter 43:2)

交流

He who knows the Tao does not care to speak about it;
he who is ever ready to speak about it does not know it.

(Chapter 56:1)

交流

He who lightly promises is sure to keep but little faith; he who is continually thinking things easy is sure to find them difficult. Therefore the sage sees difficulty even in what seems easy, and so never has any difficulties.

(Chapter 63:3)

交流

My words are very easy to know, and very easy to practise; but there is no one in the world who is able to know and able to practise them.

(Chapter 70:1)

交流

There is an originating and all-comprehending principle in my words, and an authoritative law for the things which I enforce. It is because they do not know these, that men do not know me.

(Chapter 70:2)

交流

Words that are strictly true seem to be paradoxical.

(Chapter 78:4)

交流

Sincere words are not fine; fine words are not sincere.
Those who are skilled in the Tao do not dispute about it;
the disputatious are not skilled in it.

(Chapter 81:1)

用意

Heaven is long-enduring and earth continues long.
The reason why heaven and earth are able to endure
and continue thus long is because they do not
live of, or for, themselves.
This is how they are able to continue and endure.

(Chapter 7:1)

用意

The movement of the Tao
By contraries proceeds;
And weakness marks the course
Of Tao's mighty deeds.

(Chapter 40:1)

用意

He who devotes himself to learning seeks from day to day to increase his knowledge; he who devotes himself to the Tao seeks from day to day to diminish his doing.

(Chapter 48:1)

用意

The sage has in the world an appearance of indecision,
and keeps his mind in a state of indifference to all.
The people all keep their eyes and ears directed to him,
and he deals with them all as his children.

(Chapter 49:3)

用意

He who acts with an ulterior purpose does harm; he who takes hold of a thing in the same way loses his hold. The sage does not act so, and therefore does no harm; he does not lay hold so, and therefore does not lose his hold.

(Chapter 64:3)

用意

The people make light of dying because of the greatness
of their labours in seeking for the means of living.
It is this which makes them think light of dying.
Thus it is that to leave the subject of living altogether
out of view is better than to set a high value on it.

(Chapter 75:3)

成功

When the work is done, and one's name is becoming distinguished, to withdraw into obscurity is the way of heaven.

(Chapter 9:2)

成功

Favour and disgrace would seem equally to be feared; honour and great calamity, to be regarded as personal conditions of the same kind.

(Chapter 13:1)

成功

The partial becomes complete; the crooked, straight;
the empty, full; the worn out, new.
He whose desires are few gets them;
he whose desires are many goes astray.

(Chapter 22:1)

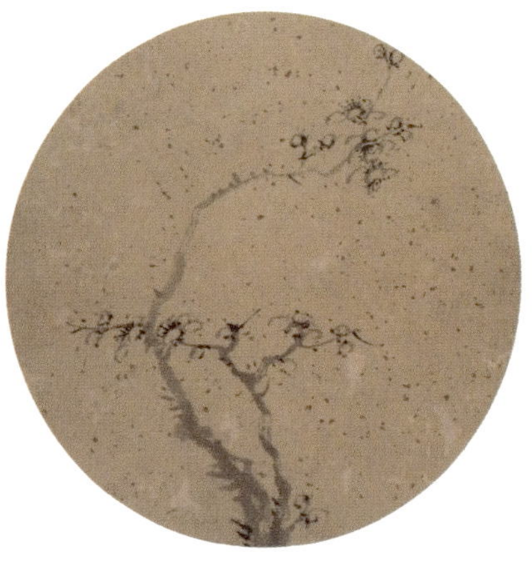

成功

Simplicity without a name
Is free from all external aim.
With no desire, at rest and still,
All things go right as of their will.

(Chapter 37:3)

成功

Those who possessed in highest degree the attributes of the Tao did not seek to show them, and therefore they possessed them in fullest measure.

(Chapter 38:1)

成功

Tao when nursed within one's self,
His vigour will make true;
And where the family it rules
What riches will accrue!

(Chapter 54:2)

成功

Misery! – happiness is to be found by its side!
Happiness! – misery lurks beneath it!
Who knows what either will come to in the end?

(Chapter 58:1)

成功

The tree which fills the arms grew from the tiniest sprout;
the tower of nine storeys rose from a small heap of earth;
the journey of a thousand li commenced with a single step.

(Chapter 64:2)

領導

Therefore he who would administer the kingdom,
honouring it as he honours his own person,
may be employed to govern it, and he who would
administer it with the love which he bears to his own
person may be entrusted with it.

(Chapter 13:3)

領導

He who displays himself does not shine; he who asserts his own views is not distinguished; he who vaunts himself does not find his merit acknowledged; he who is self-conceited has no superiority allowed to him.

(Chapter 24)

領導

The unwrought material, when divided and distributed, forms vessels. The sage, when employed, becomes the Head of all the Officers (of government); and in his greatest regulations he employs no violent measures.

(Chapter 28:2)

領導

To those who are good to me, I am good; and to those who are not good to me, I am also good; – and thus all get to be good. To those who are sincere with me, I am sincere; and to those who are not sincere with me, I am also sincere; – and thus (all) get to be sincere.

(Chapter 49:2)

領導

A state may be ruled by (measures of) correction; weapons of war may be used with crafty dexterity; (but) the kingdom is made one's own (only) by freedom from action and purpose.

(Chapter 57:1)

領導

Governing a great state is like cooking small fish.

(Chapter 60:1)

領導

The people are difficult to govern because of the excessive agency of their superiors in governing them.
It is through this that they are difficult to govern.

(Chapter 75:2)

He who knows other men is discerning; he who knows himself is intelligent. He who overcomes others is strong; he who overcomes himself is mighty. He who is satisfied with his lot is rich; he who goes on acting with energy has a firm will.

(Chapter 33:1)

强

The soft overcomes the hard; and the weak the strong.

(Chapter 36:2)

强

The perception of what is small is the secret of clear-sightedness; the guarding of what is soft and tender is the secret of strength.

(Chapter 52:4)

强

He who has in himself abundantly the attributes of the Tao
is like an infant. Poisonous insects will not sting him;
fierce beasts will not seize him;
birds of prey will not strike him.

(Chapter 55:1)

强

Man at his birth is supple and weak; at his death, firm and strong. So it is with all things. Trees and plants, in their early growth, are soft and brittle; at their death, dry and withered.

(Chapter 76:1)

强

There is nothing in the world more soft and weak than water, and yet for attacking things that are firm and strong there is nothing that can take precedence of it; – for there is nothing so effectual for which it can be changed.

(Chapter 78:1)

正義

Man takes his law from the Earth; the Earth takes its law from Heaven; Heaven takes its law from the Tao. The law of the Tao is its being what it is.

(Chapter 25:4)

正義

What makes a great state is its being (like) a low-lying, downflowing stream; – it becomes the centre to which tend all the small states under heaven.

(Chapter 61:1)

正義

The great state only wishes to unite men together and nourish them; a small state only wishes to be received by, and to serve, the other. Each gets what it desires, but the great state must learn to abase itself.

(Chapter 61:4)

正義

It is the way of the Tao to act without thinking of acting; to conduct affairs without feeling the trouble of them; to taste without discerning any flavour; to consider what is small as great, and a few as many; and to recompense injury with kindness.

(Chapter 63:1)

正義

He whose boldness appears in his daring to do wrong, in defiance of the laws is put to death; he whose boldness appears in his not daring to do so lives on.

(Chapter 73:1)

正義

The people do not fear death; to what purpose is it to try to frighten them with death? If the people were always in awe of death, and I could always seize those who do wrong, and put them to death, who would dare to do wrong?

(Chapter 74:1)

正義

The people suffer from famine because of the multitude
of taxes consumed by their superiors.
It is through this that they suffer famine.

(Chapter 75:1)

正義

It is the Way of Heaven to diminish superabundance, and to supplement deficiency. It is not so with the way of man. He takes away from those who have not enough to add to his own superabundance.

(Chapter 77:2)

正義

In the Way of Heaven, there is no partiality of love;
it is always on the side of the good man.

(Chapter 79:3)

正義

In a little state with a small population, I would so order it, that, though there were individuals with the abilities of ten or a hundred men, there should be no employment of them; I would make the people, while looking on death as a grievous thing, yet not remove elsewhere to avoid it.

(Chapter 80:1)

He who would assist a lord of men in harmony with the Tao will not assert his mastery in the kingdom by force of arms. Such a course is sure to meet with its proper return.

(Chapter 30:1)

Now arms, however beautiful, are instruments of evil omen, hateful, it may be said, to all creatures. Therefore they who have the Tao do not like to employ them.

(Chapter 31:1)

A skilful commander strikes a decisive blow, and stops. He does not dare by continuing his operations to assert and complete his mastery.

(Chapter 30:3)

兵戈

Gentleness is sure to be victorious even in battle, and firmly to maintain its ground. Heaven will save its possessor, by his very gentleness protecting him.

(Chapter 67:4)

He who in Tao's wars has skill
Assumes no martial port;
He who fights with most goodwill
To rage makes no resort.

(Chapter 68)

兵戈

A master of the art of war has said,
'I do not dare to be the host (to commence the war);
I prefer to be the guest (to act on the defensive).
I do not dare to advance an inch; I prefer to retire a foot.'

(Chapter 69:1)

There is no calamity greater than lightly engaging in war. To do that is near losing the gentleness which is so precious. Thus it is that when opposing weapons are actually crossed, he who deplores the situation conquers.

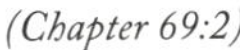

[…] he who relies on the strength of his forces does not conquer; and a tree which is strong will fill the out-stretched arms, and thereby invites the feller.

(Chapter 76:3)

The Tao is (like) the emptiness of a vessel; and in our employment of it we must be on our guard against all fulness. How deep and unfathomable it is, as if it were the Honoured Ancestor of all things!

(Chapter 4:1)

The Tao produces all things and nourishes them; it produces them and does not claim them as its own; it does all, and yet does not boast of it; it presides over all, and yet does not control them. This is what is called 'The mysterious Quality' of the Tao.

(Chapter 10:3)

The grandest forms of active force
From Tao come, their only source.

(Chapter 21)

The Tao, considered as unchanging, has no name.

(Chapter 32:1)

The great Tao (or way) is very level and easy;
but people love the byways.

(Chapter 53:2)

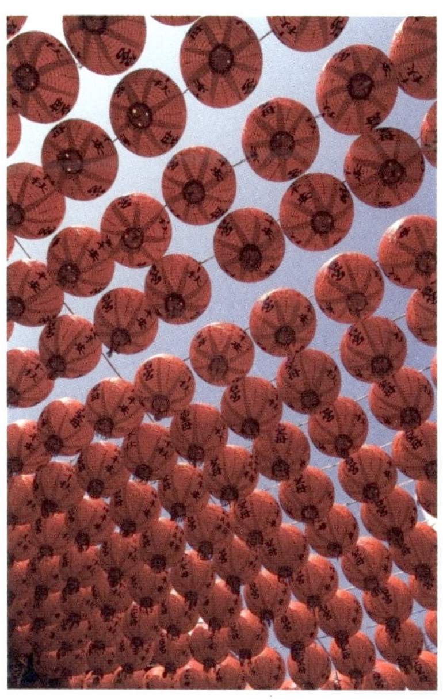

All the world says that, while my Tao is great, it yet appears to be inferior to other systems of teaching. Now it is just its greatness that makes it seem to be inferior. If it were like any other system, for long would its smallness have been known!

(Chapter 67:1)

May not the Way or Tao of Heaven be compared to the method of bending a bow? The part of the bow which was high is brought low, and what was low is raised up.

(Chapter 77:1)

Picture Credits

Alamy: 31 (Tao Wu), 34 (piemags), 45 (stockphotoready), 58 (Album), 79 (Mikel Bilbao Gorostiaga Travels), 80 (Granger Historical Picture Archive), 90 (Charles O. Cecil), 91 (The Picture Art Collection), 93 (mauritius images GmbH), 94 (CNP Collection)

Creative Commons Attribution 4.0 International license: 88 (Wellcome Collection)

Dreamstime: 10 (Shaiith), 11 (Steveheap), 12 (Hpphoto), 14 (In Sung Choi), 15 (Pisut Konepun), 17 (Ajn), 18 (Abraham219004), 19 (Kari Høglund), 22 (Kickboy24), 23 (Alex Bramwell), 25 (Aleksandr Goncharenko), 29 (Bernd Juergens), 33 (Michel Arnault), 60 (Johann Helgason), 70 (Elena Elisseeva), 72 (Huang Huang Jian), 76 (Vvoevale)

MET Museum: 24 (Yashima Gakutei), 26 (Yashima Gakutei), 28 (Sesson Shūkei), 37 (Unidentified artist), 38 (Unidentified artist), 40 (Sekishō Shōan), 41 (Unidentified artist), 43 (Deng Yu), 47 (Li Kui), 48 (Gift of Florance Waterbury), 49 (Liang Yuwei), 51 (Gift of Fong Chow), 52 (Tang Yifen), 53 (Ma Lin), 54 (Shitao), 55 (John D. Rockefeller Jr), 59 (B. Y. Lam Fund and Friends of Asian Art Gifts), 61 (Abby Aldrich Rockefeller), 62 (Rogers Fund), 63 (Gong Gu), 64 (Miao), 65 (Charlotte C. and John C. Weber Collection), 66 (Fang Congyi), 67 (Qiao Bin), 68 (Friends of Asian Art Gifts), 69 (Ermolaev Alexander), 71 (After Xia Gui), 73 (Fei Qinghu), 74 (Xiao Yuncong), 75 (Zhao Mengfu), 77 (James C. Y. Watt), 85 (The Dillon Fund Gift), 87 (Rogers Fund and Fletcher Fund), 89 (John Stewart Kennedy Fund)

Public Domain: 20, 27 (Tomáš Páv), 56 (American Museum of Natural History), 82, 84 (MondoMostre), 86, 95 (Through China with a camera)

Shutterstock: 8 (Luisa Puccini), 9 (siriwat wongchana), 13 (lowpower225), 16 (Nejron Photo), 21 (lemaret pierrick), 30 (Diana Taliun), 32 (salajean), 35 (Neveditsyna Elena), 36 (Dario Pautasso), 39 (Siwapreecha Siwaphatsakun), 42 (Xita), 44 (Focus Pix), 46 (Yavuz Sariyildiz), 50 (GuoZhongHua), 57 (jurgal), 78 (Giusparta), 81 (aphotostory), 83 (lilyling1982), 92 (WeiShen)